I0828177

FINISHING LINE PRESS
www.finishinglinepress.com

# Nothing Left to Fix

*poems by*

January Pearson

*Finishing Line Press*
Georgetown, Kentucky

# Nothing Left to Fix

ISBN 979-8-89990-391-5 First Edition


ACKNOWLEDGMENTS

I would like to thank the editors of the following journals for publishing my work. A few of the poems have been slightly modified from their original form or given new titles.

*Los Angeles Review*: "Clouds"
*Tabula Poetica: The Journal of Poetry and Poetics*: "St Joseph's X-Ray Report" and "Book of Remedies"
*Poetry South*: "For Starfish"
*Rust & Moth*: "Routine"
*Pittsburg Poetry Review*: "Ballet Lessons"
*Mockingheart Review*: "Sacraments"
*Notre Dame Review*: "Prayer along Crystal Cove" and "Gravesite"
*The Cape Rock*: "Imprint"
*Valparaiso Poetry Review*: "No Telling"
*2River*: "After" and "Seven"
*Calyx*: "Six Months Today"

Publisher: Leah Huete de Maines
Editor: Christen Kincaid
Cover Art: American Valley Drawing, by Annie White
Author Photo: Audrey Pearson
Cover Design: Elizabeth Maines McCleavy

Order online: www.finishinglinepress.com
also available on amazon.com

Author inquiries and mail orders:
Finishing Line Press
PO Box 1626
Georgetown, Kentucky 40324
USA

# Contents

*For my dad*

## Dust

*People can get Valley Fever by breathing in dust...*
—California Department of Health

Out in the Antelope Valley,
sand stretches to the cloudless sky,
mounds swirl with dust
made of pollen, skin cells,
browned grass, singed bits
of meteorite—dust upwelling
in blooms sick with disease
carried through the parched air.
The same dust God used
to create Adam. How these tiny
particles have the strength to heft
this fever and sabotage
the man standing at the gas station,
daydreaming about this unplanned
road trip with his wife, filling
their old car with gas, whistling
to the radio.

## Clouds

The pulmonologist doesn't know.
My father's lungs, filled with clouds—
the kind that hurry toward you
as a warning. He doesn't know why
my father can't catch his breath, why
water floods the small space.
He sighs for lack of words. My father
is propped on his white hospital bed
at a 90-degree angle, the clean
air around him untranslatable—
the way soft bunches of cumulus seem tangible
until you're close enough to touch them.

**Valley** (n.)—A depression between two hills. When there is no rain, the hills may be fringed with blue. The Kalalau Valley frames the ocean with emerald and amber, shaped like a soup bowl. In the winter, some valleys become a slope for children in puffy coats riding plastic sleds. Every fall, I visit valleys in Northern California flecked with yellow aspens. There are other kinds. Some form at the bottom of the ocean. Others on the drylands where the earth is breaking apart. When they say *she's going through a valley*, it means she's blue. Almost no one has heard of the valley that is a fever. Not even the doctors. It's called Valley Fever because it inhabits dusty places like the Antelope Valley. This kind isn't beautiful. The flat area between the hills is lower than usual. Sometimes when you're in a valley, you don't even know it. Sometimes you know and think of the psalmist who understood its shadows. My dad knew. His lasted so long, we thought there was no way out. But he kept insisting most valleys have a river.

**St Joseph's Hospital X-Ray**

His hip bone is luminous
on the shadowy film,
edges blurred around the femur
where fine white lines bloom
into a grey clearing, even
the round bone in the socket
shattered to fragments,
          shards of          opal pebbles
flecks of          white sea glass
          broken          sand dollars
                    chipped          porcelain teacup
elephant          tusk     slivers
          icicles     flaked          and crushed
                    threads of bright     dust     trailing a comet

**For Starfish**

whose limbs bloom like perennials

For the opah's silver scales, all the fish sequined in resilience

For taproots knotted deep in the earth, anchoring
hickories from sleeting wind

For rivers and streams, every blue rivulet guiding rain
to the ocean, for the warmth that gleams
the surface, sending water droplets to clouds

For a ladybug's crimson helmet, the beetle's black shield,
sepals circling camellia buds, the honeycomb's latticework

Thank you for the cell wall sealing in its intelligence

For skin that grows over a wound
and bones written with the wisdom to mend

For the doctor's skilled hands and plastic mysteries
repairing shattered hip bones

For the seventy-year old woman who sleeps
in the hospital chair overnight, spooning
sweet potatoes to her husband, her slender arms
barely strong enough to lift him

## Routine

Turning his chin toward her,
she lathers his face,
then dips the razor
into a bowl of warm water.
She begins cheekbone
to neckline, a straight path
between white heaps
as though clearing fresh snow.
As instructed, he flattens
his upper lip, and she works
in short strokes from one side
to the other until his skin
is clean. Even though he sees
only his children, the specialists,
and the occasional visitor,
she insists on this routine.
4 pm each day before supper
and then the evening news.
This is something she can do.

## Ballet Lessons

She used to say ballet saved her from the crows
pecking at her bedroom window, from her father
who disappeared, like grass clippings in a storm.
For hours she practiced, stretching muscles and limbs
until she could fold herself over like a sheet, softening
the taut tendons to steady the trembling inside her.
*You must wear down the sole to get better,*
her teacher would tell her in the mirror's
reflection. My mother perfected the arabesque,
the tendu, rubbing her ballet shoe back and forth
along the wooden floor until her shoe tore.
Now, at the kitchen counter, she steadies my father
by the gait belt around a chest hollow
as though the wind fell out of him.
She instructs, first position, plié. He inches
each heel into place, thin legs bending
and quivering to straighten. Stubble dusts his face,
a bobby pin sweeps strands of hair
from his eyes. She shows him how to point
and lift the leg in a développé. He strains to aim
his swollen foot and draw it back along the tile
to first position. They practice until
he leans into her. You must wear down
the sole to get better. She holds his ankle
above the running sock, drags his sickled foot
across the floor again and again.

## The Book of Remedies

Mornings, she gave him Greek yogurt
sprinkled with rose hips and red clovers.
If he wanted ice cream, she mixed in lion's mane
and rubbed his cracked skin with freshly cut
aloe she grew in her garden. When the salt
in his blood evaporated and he forgot his name,
she drove for miles to the western shores
for bucketfuls of ocean. When he kept
losing weight, she'd infuse his peanut-butter shake
with dust from a collapsed star.
The doctor told her none of this
would work. But she traveled seven nights
through endless valleys to the golden dunes
for the bluest mirage she could find.

## Sacraments

The nurses visit you like priests
offering litanies of Latin cures

and Dixie cups of sacraments,
promises of life that are forever

failing while you search for words,
having lost the strength to hold

a thought, remember today
is Sunday, or the names you knew

by heart. What you know now
is this room of sunless light,

its incessant hum of machines
and vining cords, not the purpling

heather in the cool air
or the green scent of trimmed

grass, but this bleached morning,
and the red beat of your heart

monitor, a wren's low chirp
in the fields of snow.

**Repairs**

After his knees ached for years,
he finally went in to get them fixed.
The doctors said it would be "easy peasy"—
just a matter of trimming the old bone
and making it new.

Next, it was his skin.
They had to take some out
and put some back in. Skin from his
bottom, skin from his belly, snipped
and then tucked back into the holes
on his chin, sewn into the divot
on the cusp of his ear.

Years later,
they added a battery, the size
of a snail shell, to keep his heart
pumping.

When they went in
for his brain, they inserted a small
plastic cup beneath his skull
for teaspoons of medicine.

After that, he said, *The good news is*
*there's nothing left to fix.*

## Prayer Along Crystal Cove

Let the flecks of sea glass
find me this winter,

opal and crimson embers
jeweled along the shore—

not only the sweep of stars
quilting the sky,

or the flare of poppies
illuminating the hills,

but the twitch of a dove's head,
glint of its onyx eye.

Guide me to the tambourine call
of shorebirds, but also

to the procession of ants,
quiet as dust. Lift my eyes

to the terns tilting in the breeze,
sewn webbing of feet,

feathers threaded to bone,
or the blue stillness between

branch and scalloped leaf.
When seasons of fog

turn the world colorless,
let me attend to the hidden

thrums along cresting waves,
water rippling mosaics

of light, sea foam strewn
in strings of pearls.

**Seven**

Seven meant complete to the ancients, which also means plenty. Seven loaves and a few fish fed thousands on a grassy hill one afternoon. The basket of our brain can hold seven bits of new information. Seven continents stay afloat on the grey-blue ocean. It's also true that plenty means enough: his illness lasted seven years. Or my mother gave him seven + seven medications morning and night. He learned to walk, fell, and learned to walk again for those years of hospital beds and needle pricks and surgeries. All this went on until he turned seventy. His mother believed illness was a sin. She counted seven deadly ones. Someone else said we should forgive seventy times seven, which is the same as two mirrors reflecting into infinity. In some respects, having enough means your belly is full. In another, it's how much rain one shoe can hold.

## Despite Everything

You notice the potato vine's shoots,
how they strive against gravity
and wind. You may not feel like looking up
when the doctor's visit crumples hope,
but there's still this Wednesday morning,
and the pink tongue of your dog licking
your ankles. Hot tea with cream.
Sliced oranges fresh from your tree.
Your granddaughter toddles to you
in her dirty socks and presses her hands
on your knees. You know what she wants.
And so you sing the "ABC Song,"
throat hoarse, catching on the *k*, throwing
you into a coughing fit. She claps and bounces,
radiant with a joy so elemental that despite
everything, you can't help but feel it.

## Visiting Him in the Hospital After 17 Days on the Ventilator

*How are you, Dad?* I ask.
He clenches his bruised fingers
into a thumbs up.

## Imprint

He'd pop off
the top of the Skoal can
and tuck a small mound
under his lip, then slip the tin
into his pocket. Sweet
bitterness like burnt sugar,
an aroma worn into his
VW bug, his calloused hands,
clean cotton shirts.
At night, I'd see his jeans
crumpled on the floor, imprint
weathered into the denim,
the way some impressions
form outlines of the past,
only kinder, old cloth
fading and lightening,
stitched threads
pressed in a circle,
softening.

## No Telling

Just the other day
I saw the snow's soft
stars cover the lawn,
their lithe floating,
each feathery crystal luffed
and loosened by the briefest
puff of air, lighter
than water, slightly
brighter than sunlight.

Then nightfall's
sharp drop to chill,
every droplet etched
sprigs of grass sharpened,
a leaf's brittle skeleton,
and the porch steps glassy
in the solid now.

When the water will run again,
trickling along bricks,
streaming against rocks,
or for how long
there is no telling.

## Gravesite

A man kneels in pressed polos
and khakis, his body folded over

as though in prayer,
but his hands move briskly

over the stone, brushing dirt
and pebbles that cover the name

of his beloved. He sweeps away
each grass clipping and speck

of dust until the stone is clear,
his fingers small brooms

in this enormous room of loss.

## After

Some think the soul resides in the head.
Some think it fits snugly in the part
that loves and aches. When it escapes
does it leave a small absence? Once,
a physician determined the soul weighs
twenty-one grams—about the weight
of a hedgehog, which is about the size
of a heart. The widow at the table disagrees.
The empty place is the size of a tornado,
which is made of wind, another word
for soul. On the inside, a tornado is calm,
the opposite of everything around it.

## Conveyer

Once you begin plodding along grief's black surface,
your body heavy with memories,
you hardly notice it's there. It simply moves you
through the cavernous rooms
of people hurrying, as though nothing has changed.
The sky is still cloudless. Airplanes still lift
into the blue. People behind you grow smaller
at a clip you're not comfortable with.
Sometimes, you want to struggle against
the forward motion, turn back to where you began,
but you stay where you are, sometimes walking,
sometimes falling, as it takes you.

**Six Months Today**

I haven't listened
to his voicemails yet,
the dozen instances of *Dad*
still lighting up my screen,
the minutes and seconds
of each message illuminated,
a column of *Dads*
a bridge to before,
the sound of his voice
coming through a closed dor.

## The Living Air

As night shrouds
and the white birches
grow black
as a sealed box,
I can't help
but think of death.
The flutter of wings
quieting. The living
air chilly. Night comes
like a diagnosis.
Yet, the lighthouse
of the moon still turns on
its faithful lamp.
Even the dark curtain
of the sky
lets through a few
pinpricks of light.

## What if death

is hard snow softening
in the sun. Every broken
thing undone. A *to be* verb
made concrete. Tight braid
of hair released. Light
after an eclipsed moon.
New skin over a deep
wound. An afternoon nap
on an old comfortable chair.
A waking up. Not here,
but somewhere.

**January Pearson**'s poetry has appeared in *Tahoma Literary Review, Calyx, Los Angeles Review, Notre Dame Review,* and other publications. She lives in Southern California with her husband and two daughters.

www.ingramcontent.com/pod-product-compliance
Lightning Source LLC
LaVergne TN
LVHW091813110826
845146LV00006B/1227

* 9 7 9 8 8 9 9 9 0 3 9 1 5 *